Explaining Faith

Colin Urquhart

Sovereign World

All Scripture quotations are from the New International Version
© Copyright 1973, 1978 International Bible Society.
Published by Hodder & Stoughton.

ISBN: 1 85240 085 4

SOVEREIGN WORLD LIMITED
P.O. Box 777, Tonbridge, Kent TN11 9XT, England.

Typeset and printed in the UK by Sussex Litho Ltd, Chichester, West Sussex.

Contents

1

Explaining Faith

Faith is not trying to believe something uncertain or even impossible.

> *Now faith is being sure of what we hope for and certain of what we do not see.*　　　　　　　　　　(Hebrews 11:1)

Faith is being sure and certain. When faith operates the impossible becomes possible. There are many things about which we are sure and certain; faith is a principle by which we live every day. We take certain things for granted. When you sit down on a chair, for example, you expect it to support your weight. You do not expect it to collapse. When you go for a walk you do not anticipate that the ground will give way beneath your feet. In normal circumstances you breathe all day long without even thinking about whether there is sufficient oxygen in the air. So when you are sure and certain about something you do not even give it very much thought. You simply know and accept that a certain thing is true.

You can have faith in your feelings, in which case your feelings will govern your life.

You can have faith in your fears and be paralysed into inactivity.

You can have faith in some kind of political philosophy, in which case you will devote yourself to such ideology.

You can have faith in others and often be disappointed.

Or you can have faith in God and learn that He is utterly trustworthy in every situation.

Different Kinds of Faith

The New Testament speaks of different kinds of faith. There is:

A) *Justifying Faith:* The faith that brings us into a living relationship with God through Jesus Christ. This is the faith that justifies us, makes us righteous and acceptable in God's sight.

B) *Doctrinal Faith:* embodies what we believe about God. The Bible reveals God's nature to us. He is Lord. He is love. He is almighty. He is holy etc.

C) *Living or Dynamic Faith:* The faith we are to live by, day by day. Because we believe God is the kind of God He is, we therefore expect Him to do certain things, honouring the promises He gives us in His Word.

We are going to look at these three kinds of faith.

2

The Faith that Justifies

The gospel about Jesus Christ is good news. But there is no good news without bad news. The bad news is that all have sinned and fallen short of the glory of God. Every person is born with a sinful nature, which means that he or she will inevitably sin.

By comparison God is holy, righteous and perfect in all His ways. Clearly an unholy, unrighteous, imperfect sinner cannot be at one with a holy, righteous and perfect God. Something has to happen to a person before he can be in a living relationship with God. His sins need to be forgiven. He needs to be made righteous in God's sight, assured that God has completely accepted him.

This is possible because of all that Jesus Christ did on the cross. God became man in Jesus. He taught about the Kingdom of God, or the Kingdom of heaven, as a present reality as well as something for which we hope in the future. He began His ministry with this proclamation:

"The hour has come, the Kingdom of God is at hand. Repent and believe the good news."

Repent and Believe

To repent is to turn away from your sin and receive forgiveness from God in order to be made acceptable in His sight. This is not simply being sorry for sin. Many people are sorry for their sins without turning away from them.

We can receive God's Kingdom as a gift when we have turned away from our sin and put our faith in what Jesus did for us on the cross. He did not only teach about the Kingdom, but made it possible for us to enter that Kingdom and for God to place that Kingdom within us now.

For us to be forgiven it was necessary for Jesus to make a sacrifice of His life on the cross. God's just judgement upon sin is that the sinner deserves to die, to be eternally separated from Him. And heaven is a place for saints, not sinners.

No man can make himself forgiven in God's sight. Nobody can earn his way into the Kingdom of God. Somebody had to bear the punishment that each of us deserves, that just punishment of death. So Jesus died on our behalf. He suffered the punishment we deserve. He offered to the Father a sinless life on behalf of sinners, a perfect life on behalf of the imperfect, a righteous life on behalf of the unrighteous, a holy life on behalf of the unholy.

He is our substitute, the one who took our place and the punishment we deserve. God's justice is satisfied by such an offering made on our behalf.

To believe in what Jesus did on the cross is to accept that Jesus did these things for you personally. He died in your place to take your punishment on Himself. This makes it possible for your sins to be forgiven, for you to be made righteous and acceptable in God's sight, for you to receive salvation so that you will not be condemned but will receive the gift of eternal life. This makes it possible for God to give you the gift of His Kingdom and for you to live in a relationship of love and unity with God, knowing that He is your Father and you are His child.

A person has to confess his sins to Jesus to experience forgiveness. He has to surrender his life to God in order to receive the life of Jesus. As you give your life to Jesus, so He gives His life to you. That giving of your life to Jesus is the act of faith that leads to your new birth, when you receive a new life from God. He never turns away from those who come to Him asking for forgiveness and surrendering their lives to Him.

A person can only become a Christian through an act of faith. In response to that faith God does His work of grace, giving to the believer everything He has to give.

The Fruit of Faith

When you repent and put your faith in Jesus and all He did on the cross, God does a number of amazing things in your life. The New Testament tells us about these things and we shall be looking at many of them in further detail later on. It takes the rest of your Christian life to learn how to live in the good of what He did on the day you became a Christian. That was the day you were born again and made one with Jesus:

> *And you also were included in Christ when you heard the word of truth, the gospel of your salvation. Having believed, you were marked in him with a seal, the promised Holy Spirit, who is a deposit guaranteeing our inheritance.*
>
> (Ephesians 1:13-14a)

These are truths for you when you were born again:

> *He forgave you all your sins.*
> *You are no longer under the condemnation you deserve.*
> *Your old life without God has passed away; it no longer exists.*
> *You are no longer controlled by the sinful nature with which you were born.*
> *You have now become a new creation.*
> *The Spirit of God has given you a new spiritual birth.*
> *You are set free from the power of the devil.*
> *God has given you the gift of His Kingdom.*
> *He has planted His Kingdom in you like a seed.*
> *You have the gift of eternal life.*
> *God has placed you in His Son.*
> *Jesus lives in you.*
> *You can now live your life in Jesus and know that He is living His life out in you.*

You are now a child of God, a son of God, an inheritor with Jesus of everything that God has to give.

All these things became true for you simply because you *put your faith* in what Jesus did for you on the cross. You believe in the fact that God gave His life for you to reconcile you to Himself. That kind of faith makes you sure and certain that God loves you, has forgiven you and will always care for you. This is the faith that justifies.

Jesus: The Only Way of Salvation

In his writings, Paul makes it very clear that there is no other way by which anybody can be saved except through faith in Jesus Christ. The actual work of salvation is a work of God's grace. Grace means that God gives His everything to those who deserve nothing. But He gives that grace in response to our faith.

There is no other name under heaven by which a man can be saved than the name, Jesus Christ. There is no other saviour or religion that can bring man into a relationship with God. Jesus Himself said:

> *I am the way, the truth and the life. No one comes to the Father except by me.* (John 14:6)

Called to Live by Faith

Just as you can only become a Christian through faith, so you can only live as a Christian by faith. It is not a question of making an initial act of faith and then trying to please God by the works you perform. Faith has to be a continual trusting in God, and in the promises He gives to His children. They can then live in His grace, His continual giving of Himself and His riches to them.

Many misunderstand the salvation God gives us through Jesus. They think that all that is required is an initial decision by which they make some form of commitment to God, which guarantees their eternal destiny. This is far from the case. Jesus does not talk about making acts of commitment at evangelistic meetings, or at any other time. He talks about being born again and becoming a disciple. When he or she is born again the believer becomes a new person and has a new nature: Christ in him or her. Anyone who is truly born again desires to please the Lord. He loves Jesus and wants to obey Him. There is ample evidence of new birth by the changes in his life, his character and his priorities – even though he is not immediately made perfect and is still able to sin and please himself.

Jesus made it clear that if you love Him you will obey His commandments. If you are born again, you will live in relationship with Christ. In the Bible salvation is a continuous process which begins when you are born again. You have been saved, are being saved and will be saved. You are to work out your salvation with fear and trembling, not wanting to displease your Lord. You are able to live in the good of the promises God has made, looking forward to the time when you will be completely transformed into His likeness.

The whole process of salvation is a continual work of God's grace in your life in response to the faith you have put in Jesus.

3

Doctrinal Faith

The Bible tells us who God really is; His character and personality. Many people say they have their own ideas of God; but that is like creating a god of your own. No such god could possibly save you, care for you or answer your prayers in miraculous ways.

It is important, therefore, that whatever ideas we have about God are tested by the revelation of who He is in Scripture.

God is not an idea. He is not a mind. No one can think their way into relationship with Him by their rational thought processes. Because God is greater than we are, His thoughts and ways much higher than ours, it is only possible to know Him by revelation. The Bible gives us that revelation. Here we can only briefly summarise some of the main characteristics of God. It is important for us to do this because we cannot live by faith if we do not know the one in whom we have faith. God will always act according to His nature so it is important for us to know what that nature is.

God is Holy

This is His essential nature. Immediately we are presented with a problem, for it is impossible for us to describe adequately what it means to say that He is holy. If we could describe His holiness He would not be holy. The nearest we can get in a brief definition of His holiness is to say that He is whole, complete and perfect in Himself. Therefore He alone is worthy of worship and praise.

God is Righteous

He always does what is right. Righteousness can only be understood in reference to God. He is the standard by which all our actions are judged. He cannot do anything wrong because He is the one who makes the rules. He will never act in opposition to His nature. When your ways are in harmony with His ways you walk in righteousness. When your ways disagree with His ways you sin.

He is Love

Although He is always right, God always loves. He loves all He has made, even those who reject His love. He deals lovingly with those who turn to Him with repentance and faith by forgiving them, making them His children and giving them the rich inheritance of His Kingdom.

He is Merciful

God's forgiveness is an expression of His mercy. He does not deal with us as our sins deserve. In His mercy He has provided Jesus to be the sacrifice for our sins.

He is Gracious

We could never deserve to receive from God. Everything He gives us and does for us is a work of His grace. He graciously gives us all things.

He is Just

He always deals justly with His children, not according to what we deserve but according to what Jesus has done for us. In His justice He forgives our sins whenever we confess them and cleanses us from all unrighteousness. He does not punish us for our sins because Jesus has already suffered our punishment.

He is the Judge

There will come the time when every person will be judged. Those who put their faith in Jesus do not need to fear the judgement, because their eternal security is in the one who gave His life for them. But those who have rejected Jesus have every right to fear the eternal judgement they will face.

In scripture the phrase *"I am"* is used to describe God's nature. He is described as our Salvation, our Shield, our Deliverer, for example.

When Jesus came to earth, He also used this phrase *"I am"* to describe essential characteristics of His nature:

I am the Good Shepherd

He has come and cared for His people, to lead them out of darkness into the life of His Kingdom.

I am the Way

Jesus is the only way to salvation for man. Nobody can come to the Father except by Him.

I am the Life

True life, life in all its fullness, can only be found in Jesus. He came to give us that life in Himself. It becomes ours when we put our faith in Him.

I am the Resurrection

Jesus promises that He will raise up all those who die with faith in Him. They will live and reign with Him in glory.

God does not want us simply to believe He exists. Many non-

Christians believe there is a God, so do demons! It is what we believe about God that matters.

> *He is the Creator.*
> *He is not an impersonal force, but a Spirit with personality who can be known as Father.*
> *He has revealed Himself, His nature and personality, through His Son, Jesus Christ.*
> *He loves.*
> *He forgives and saves those who put their trust in Him.*
> *He gives eternal life to those who believe in Him.*
> *He answers the prayers of those who have faith in Him.*

4

Living by Dynamic Faith

Jesus spent three and a half years with the twelve disciples and taught many other disciples as well. He constantly trained them to trust in God's supernatural power. *Faith in the true God releases His supernatural activity into our lives.* His power is greater than any natural force or energy. He is able to intervene in our daily circumstances and change situations. He is able to heal bodies because He is greater than all He has made.

There is a certain dimension of faith which many Christians have never enjoyed, even though they may be born again and filled with the Holy Spirit.

Those who are born again have a personal relationship with Him. Those who are filled with the Spirit have experience of the inner working of God in their lives. Yet this does not necessarily mean that they trust God's Word as the guiding principle in their lives.

Double-Minded

If they do not live by faith they try to acquire faith when in a difficult situation or in desperate need. Often they are disappointed and make such comments as, "I really try to believe; I want to trust God." They may recognise that nothing is impossible for Him, but without trusting Him to answer personal need with a miracle. They may know that He is the Healer and that by the stripes of Jesus they are healed, but not have confidence in His desire to heal them.

Those who live in this way have a fluctuating faith. Sometimes their faith in God seems to be strong, but often they are double-minded: "Will God answer, or won't He? Will He do this, or won't He? Does He want to heal me, or doesn't He?"

James says that a double-minded man is unstable in all his ways and cannot expect to receive *anything* from God. **Clearly He wants us to have a steady confidence in Him which is not affected by external circumstances. Such faith changes the circumstances.**

Word and Fruit

There is a very definite dimension of faith which God wants **all** believers to enjoy. In scripture, faith comes in two ways:-

a)   By hearing the Word of God;

b)   As a gift of the Holy Spirit.

If you are going to live in the faith dimension, you must uncompromisingly accept the authority of God's Word. You need to recognise that if God's Word says one thing and you say another, someone has to be wrong. **Learn to submit your thinking to the attitudes revealed in scripture.** Believe what God says about you and your circumstances rather than what your own feelings or reason tell you.

God is not unreasonable; He is beyond reason. Reason deals with the natural; God is supernatural. So the reason cannot fully comprehend God or the way in which He is prepared to act in our lives.

> *The Holy Spirit who lives in you as a believer is the Spirit of truth. He encourages you to believe the authority of God's Word in every situation.*

5

Faith in Jesus' Ministry

Jesus Himself lived by faith. He trusted His Father in every circumstance. He said that He could do nothing on His own; He only did the things He saw His Father doing. He spoke no words of His own, but only the words His Father gave Him to speak.

Jesus Raises the Dead

Jesus shows that to live by faith is to live in dependence on the Father. We see an example of this in the incident concerning Lazarus. When Jesus heard about his imminent death He did not rush immediately to the scene. Instead, He made the first of a series of significant faith statements:

"This sickness will not end in death."   (John 11:4)

This was not only prophetic, it demonstrated Jesus' determination that Satan would not have the victory in this situation.

When Jesus made it clear to the disciples that Lazarus had died, He made another faith statement:

"I am going there to wake him up."   (John 11:11)

Jesus is dependent on God's supernatural power being revealed through Him. So He does not look at the situation from a purely natural viewpoint. His Spirit, rather than His reason is in control in the situation. Jesus made another faith statement when Martha met Him:

"Your brother will rise again."   (John 11:23)

Jesus always lived His own teaching. He taught the disciples to believe that they had already received the answer to their prayer and it would be given to them. Clearly Jesus did this Himself. So when He stood before the tomb, He prayed:

> *"Father, I thank you that you have heard me. I knew that you always hear me."* (John 11:41-42)

Each of these faith statements indicates what He believed would happen. He believed the Father had already given the answer before He commanded Lazarus to come out of the tomb. He did not go to Bethany with despair or death in His heart. He was confident in what His Father would do in raising His friend from the dead.

Jesus Heals

God's supernatural power overcomes natural limitations.
Jesus fed more than five thousand with five loaves and two small fishes. He enabled Peter to walk on water and to find a coin in a fish. He commanded the wind and the waves to obey Him.

People constantly sought Jesus for healing. On many occasions, He told them that they received their healing in response to faith.

> *Some men brought to him a paralytic, lying on a mat. **When Jesus saw their faith,** he said to the paralytic, "Take heart, son; your sins are forgiven."* (Matthew 9:2)

> *Jesus turned and saw her. "Take heart, daughter," he said, **"your faith has healed you."** And the woman was healed from that moment.* (Matthew 9:22)

> *Then he touched their eyes and said, **"According to your faith will it be done to you."*** (Matthew 9:29)

> *Then Jesus answered, **"Woman, you have great faith! Your***

request is granted." And her daughter was healed from that very hour. (Matthew 15:28)

*Jesus said to the woman, "**Your faith has saved you;** go in peace."* (Luke 7:50)

*Then he said to him, "Rise and go; **your faith has made you well."*** (Luke 17:19)

Nazareth was the only place where Jesus could not perform many miracles. This was because of *"their lack of faith"* (Mark 6:5-6). And He was disappointed with His disciples whenever they lacked faith.

From Jesus' teaching, it is clear that:

Faith produces results.
Unbelief restricts God's activity.
Only you limit Him by your unbelief.
The Lord never wants to limit Himself in your experience.

Words of Authority and Power

Notice how often Jesus has to speak only a sentence to change a whole situation.

"Peace, be still", and the wind and the waves obeyed him.
"Be opened!"
"Get up and walk."
"Your sins are forgiven you."

Could such things happen today? Most certainly.

Jesus Heals Today

I was speaking at a conference in Scotland. During the early part of the conference it was a common sight to see a man being carried up the main stairs in his wheelchair. His spine had been broken in an accident. He was confined to the chair for the rest of his life.

Mid-way through the conference he attended a seminar on baptism in the Holy Spirit. He had already received this blessing but thought he would add his prayer support to those ministering. During the course of the ministry period at the end of the seminar, God told him to stand up; a physical impossibility. He heard God, believed Him and stood up, completely healed. No-one ministered to him or laid hands on him. He simply heard God speak two words.

It was a glorious sight to see him walking up those same stairs during the latter part of the conference, carrying his two small children.

God may speak such a word to you directly, or through a word of knowledge when someone is praying with you. He may simply give you a word of Scripture which you know to be His voice to you. Sometimes words of promise follow words of command. When such a word requires obedience, do what He says.

6

Faith in God's Word

Faith is a matter of choice. It is never true to say you could not believe. In every situation, you can choose either to believe the revelation of the truth of the circumstances, reason, doubt or fear. The choice is yours.

Learning to live by faith is learning to make the right choices, believing God no matter how you feel or what others say. It is difficult to live by faith if you are too concerned about the reactions of others, rather than what God thinks of you.

People who are full of faith are very positive. Even in difficult situations they can still be happy because they trust God to intervene in some way.

When people fail to put their faith in Jesus in their daily lives, they often speak negatively about themselves, others and their situation. They need to be freed from this negative unbelief by having their minds renewed according to God's Word. What God says in His Word is more real than circumstances, feelings or human thinking!

> *Heaven and earth will pass away but my words will never pass away.*　　　　　　　　　　　　　(Matthew 24:35)

The good news is that you do not have to be influenced by negative attitudes, thoughts, ideas and words. You have a choice to either concentrate on the things of the flesh (your soul and body operating independently of God) or to set your mind on things of the Spirit (dependent on God). You can choose to think the way God thinks; by learning to agree with His Word, which will give you life and peace. Or you can think according to the standards of the world, which leads to death!

God does not want you to lead a defeated, miserable life, but a life of faith in JESUS CHRIST, allowing God's Spirit to influence your mind because you believe the truth of His Word.

FREEDOM WILL COME WHEN YOU:

> *HEAR GOD'S WORD.*
> *BELIEVE GOD'S WORD.*
> *ACT ON GOD'S WORD.*

God's Word reveals who He is, what He has done for us in Jesus and what He wants of us. We have to choose whether to obey or disobey, to believe or contradict what He says.

Faith is a matter of choice

When the Spirit speaks a word of faith to your heart, you have the choice to accept or reject that word. The Holy Spirit urges you to believe and act in obedience to what God says.

> *If you hold to my teaching, you are really my disciples. Then you will know the truth and the truth will set you free.* (John 8:31-32)

If the words of Jesus are truth, anything which contradicts what He says is not true. Let us take a simple example. A Christian could be sick. He recognises the symptoms of disease in his body. The sickness may have been diagnosed by his doctor. He cannot doubt the reality of his sickness. This appears to be the truth about his condition.

A Christian is incorporated into Christ and all that Jesus did on the cross is his inheritance. God's Word clearly says, *"by his stripes we are healed"*. How can the Christian reconcile these two things?

There cannot be two contradictory truths, so the Christian has to decide which of these two conflicting things he will believe. If he claims he is healed by the stripes of Jesus, he aligns himself with the truth of God's Word. **He does not doubt the reality of the disease, but acknowledges that this is not the ultimate**

24

truth about his condition.

It is true at the natural level that he has the sickness. It is true at the spiritual or supernatural level that he is healed by the stripes of Jesus. Will he live at the natural level like any non-believer, or will he live by faith in God's supernatural provision?

God has provided for this sick believer. When he understands this, he sees that faith is not a question of asking God whether He wants to provide a particular healing or not; *it is an entering by faith into the supernatural provision God has already made.* He believes what he does not see (Hebrews 11:1).

A Christian living by dynamic faith takes hold of the truth as God reveals it, and applies it to his circumstances.

Faith comes by hearing, and hearing by the Word of God.
(Romans 10:17)

7

Hear and Believe

From cover to cover, the Bible is full of the exploits of men who heard God and believed what He said. When the Hebrews were escaping from Egypt and were trapped between the Red Sea and the pursuing Egyptian army, Moses heard God tell him to stretch out his hand over the sea and the waters would be separated, making it possible for His people to cross on dry ground. Moses believed God and acted upon His Word. So the miracle happened! **He chose not to believe the natural situation** which spelt disaster for all the Hebrews. **He chose to believe the revelation that God had given by speaking to him.**

The Egyptians had received no such revelation. When they tried to pursue the Hebrews, the waters came together and they were drowned.

God is Spirit and He will communicate with your spirit. The two principal ways in which we can hear God speak to us are:

a) Through the Scriptures
When you read your Bible, ask the Holy Spirit to declare His Word to your heart. Certain verses will leap out of the page and into your heart, as if that particular verse was not in your Bible before! **You know God has spoken to you** and that this verse or passage is relevant to you at that time. It becomes personal to you.

b) By the Holy Spirit
This can be either by hearing God directly in your own spirit or through someone else who is giving an inspired word of revelation. Whereas we know God's Word is always infallible, **we are told to test words of prophecy against the truth of scripture**. Anything which conflicts with God's Word certainly does not come from Him.

Sons of Abraham

In the Bible, those who live by faith are called sons of Abraham. He lived by faith. God spoke to him and gave him an amazing set of promises:

> *I will make you a great nation and I will bless you; I will make your name great, and you will be a blessing. I will bless those who bless you, and whoever curses you I will curse; and all peoples on earth will be blessed through you.*
> (Genesis 12:2-3)

God promised that Abraham and Sarah would have a child, even though both were long past the age of childbearing.

> *It was not through law that Abraham and his offspring received the promise that he would be heir of the world, but through the righteousness that comes by faith.* (Romans 4:13)

Paul continues to say that Abraham did not believe the circumstances but the promise that God had given him. He knew that his body was as good as dead because he was about a hundred years old and Sarah's womb was also dead. **But he did not weaken in his faith or waver through unbelief regarding God's promise. He believed totally that God had the power to do what He had said. That is genuine faith.**

When you believe what God says in His Word, regardless of the circumstances, you are indeed living by faith. It is such a temptation to believe what you see around you and to disregard what God has said. But faith believes God over and above the circumstances. It is a question of believing the faithfulness of God.

> *By faith Abraham, even though he was past age – and Sarah herself was barren – was enabled to become a father because he considered him faithful who had made the promise.* (Hebrews 11:12)

Often you will need to hold onto the promise of God against all odds. This is the way to be abundantly fruitful. In Jesus' parable of the sower, the ones who bear a hundred-fold fruit are described as those who hold fast to the Word of God with an honest and good heart.

Listening to God would be easy if it was not for the devil. When the Lord speaks He does not deceive. The enemy seeks to sow confusion in believers by speaking words that contradict the truth. He does this very subtly. His appeal is often to reason or feelings, and he likes to sow seeds of doubt about God's love.

"If God loves you, why has he allowed his to happen to you?" "How could a God of love allow you to suffer in such a way?" "Why should God heal you? There is nothing special about you."

Jesus describes him as the father of lies, a liar from the beginning, the deceiver, the accuser of the brethren, the thief who steals, kills and destroys.

Satan understands the power of faith. He will steal God's Word from you if you give him the opportunity. Jesus makes this clear in the parable of the sower. Some of the seed, which represents God's Word, fell on the path. The birds, which represent Satan, ate the seed. If you do not receive the words which God speaks to you, Satan will snatch them away. Then the promises that God made will not be fulfilled. Satan must be a fat bird because so many Christians allow him to steal from them the words that God speaks!

It is important not only to hear God's Word but to **act on it**.

> *Do not merely listen to the word, and so deceive yourselves. Do what it says. The man who looks intently into the perfect law that gives freedom, and continues to do this, not forgetting what he has heard, but doing it – he will be blessed in what he does.* (James 1:22, 25)

If faith is not accompanied by action it is dead, as thoroughly ineffective as a corpse. We need to show our faith by what we do. Having heard and believed the truth, we must act on what has been said to see the fruit we desire.

8

Knowing Who You Are
in Christ Jesus

When you put your faith in Jesus, God made you His child, placed you in Christ and gave you His Holy Spirit.

> *If anyone acknowledges that Jesus is the Son of God, God lives in him and he in God.*   (1 John 4:15)

According to your position:

> *You are in Christ and Christ is in you.*
> *You live in God and God in you.*
> *You live in the Spirit and the Spirit lives in you.*

The Lord wants to give you personal revelation of your position in Him. So you will know this to be the truth about yourself. Then you will not try to believe; you will believe.

Whether we speak of living "in God" or living "in Jesus", ultimately we mean the same thing. I was a Christian a long time before I fully understood what it was to live "in Christ". Jesus said: *"Abide in me and I in you"*. The word *"abide"* appears in the continuous tense in the Greek. Translated literally, it means *"to go on continually living in"*. God wants you to continue to live in Jesus – where He has placed you!

He has put His Spirit within you to enable you to remain "in Christ". You have been placed in Him by God's gracious act and He lives in you to enable you to live daily in His grace, in His abundant generosity towards you.

Your Inheritance in Christ

Scripture says that apart from Jesus you cannot inherit anything from God, but because you live in Jesus:

You have come to fulness of life in Him.
You have received the fulness of life Jesus came to give.

"You **have** come", not "You **will** come!" Your inheritance is not held for you in a distant and hazy future; it has already been given to you. Imagine your inheritance as a treasure chest filled with priceless jewels, which God has given you as a gift. There is little point in admiring them from a distance; God wants you to take hold of them and use them as your own. He has actually placed this treasure within you! (2 Corinthians 4:7)

You are "in Christ"; so you have the key which opens the lid to the treasure chest. Understand this basic truth: If you are in Christ Jesus, every Scripture which talks about being "in Christ" is a truth about YOU. God has taken hold of your life and put you in Christ. He wants you to live in the FULNESS of life which He has given you.

Every Spiritual Blessing

God has blessed us in Christ with every spiritual blessing in the heavenly realms. (Ephesians 1:3)

"Us" includes YOU!

He does not say "He **will** bless us" but that *"He **has** blessed us"*. Not with **"some"** spiritual blessing but with *"every"* spiritual blessing.

My God will supply every need of yours according to his riches in glory in Christ Jesus. (Philippians 4:19)

It is God's purpose to meet **your every need**! He is able and willing to do this.

The Plan from the Beginning

For he chose us in him before the creation of the world to be holy and blameless in his sight. In love, he predestined us to be adopted as his sons through Jesus Christ, in accordance with his pleasure and will. (Ephesians 1:4-5)

God had **YOU** on His mind before He created the world! This is difficult to understand with your reason. But it is a truth to believe in your heart. God planned to place **YOU** in Christ before you were born! He had **YOUR** inheritance prepared from the beginning of time!

- *He chose YOU to be His child.*
- *He chose YOU to be a co-heir with Christ.*
- *He chose YOU to be a temple of His Holy Spirit.*
- *He chose YOU to live in Him.*

He placed you in Christ Jesus when you heard the message of salvation and believed in Him. **YOU** need no longer live in doubt and fear, for God has placed His stamp of ownership on you. He has given **YOU** His Holy Spirit as a guarantee of your inheritance. **You are His! You belong to Him completely!** God wants you to know your full position in Christ. You can live in freedom from negativity. You can draw on His love, joy, strength and provision every day of your life.

What an amazing truth, that God planned such a wonderful inheritance for you before the creation of the world! It is yours. You only have to lay claim to it and live in the good of all He has chosen to do for you.

9

Crucified with Christ

Paul's testimony is:

> *I have been crucified with Christ and I no longer live, but Christ lives in me. The life I live in the body, I live by faith in the Son of God, who loved me and gave himself for me.*
> (Galatians 2:20)

What was true for Paul is true for you. You have been crucified with Christ. At the time of the crucifixion Paul was an enemy of Jesus. Yet he came to realise that when Christ died the old Saul of Tarsus died with Him.

Whatever you may have been before you put your faith personally in Jesus does not matter. That old life has been crucified with Christ. **He took your former self to the cross and you died there with Him.** God's estimate of that old self life was that it could not be corrected, improved upon, healed or made acceptable in His sight. There was only one thing to do: put it to death.

The cross was God's method of accomplishing this. You were crucified with him so that your old life, centred upon self and sin, no longer exists. **The person you are now is not the old person you used to be. Your new identity is Christ living in you.**

Your old life could not survive the cross. It could not survive death. Because that old life has been put to death you have died to all that the sinful self counted dear, a life of selfishness, worldliness, self-centredness and self-concern. The life you now live is the life of Jesus living in your body with your active co-operation.

> *May I never boast except in the cross of our Lord Jesus Christ, through which the world has been crucified to me, and I to the world.*
> (Galatians 6:14)

Because your former worldly self has been put to death, you have been crucified to the world and the world has been crucified to you. No longer are you to conform to the pattern of this world.

New Thinking

You are to be transformed by the renewing of your mind. Instead of thinking in worldly or rational terms you believe the revelation of what Christ has done for you. **Believing His Word will enable you to know His good, pleasing and perfect will.** You are not going to live as the world lives. God has empowered you to live His life, the life of Jesus in the world. You have the Holy Spirit living in you to enable you to do this.

You Have Died

For we know that our old self was crucified with him so that the body of sin might be done away with, that we should no longer be slaves to sin. (Romans 6:6)

Your old life was crucified with Christ. The person you used to be was nailed to the cross with Him. This is a fact, something of which you can be certain. You know this, not by any feelings you may have, but because God tells you in His Word. Resolve, therefore, never to forget this, but to live consciously in the fact that your old life has been nailed to the cross with Jesus and put to death. The person you were before you turned to Christ no longer exists. That old self, full of unbelief and rebellion, has been executed.

Because Jesus took you to the cross you have shared in His crucifixion. When He died, you died. That old life has no dominion or influence over you now. It has not simply been put to sleep. It is dead! So you are no longer in bondage to the person you used to be, to your former sins, evil habits and attitudes. Sin is no longer your master and your body is no longer an instrument of sin. You are not a slave to sin but a slave to righteousness.

Now if we died with Christ, we believe that we will also live with him. (Romans 6:8)

With Christ in God

Because you shared in the death of Jesus on the cross by faith, you can also live with Him now and for eternity. You can only live the new resurrection life of Jesus because you have been incorporated into His death.

For you died, and your life is now hidden with Christ in God. (Colossians 3:3)

Now you live in Him and you are united with Christ in God, seated with Him in heavenly places. Your new self is not seeking union with Christ; you are already made one with Him. You are not trying to get near to God; you already live in Him because you are united with His Son. You no longer have any identity apart from your life in Christ.

The death he died, he died to sin once for all; but the life he lives, he lives to God. In the same way, count yourselves dead to sin but alive to God in Christ Jesus. (Romans 6:10-11)

10

Count Yourself Dead

Dead to Sin

Because you have died with Christ you are now dead to the things that opposed Christ. You can live in the reality of this truth. You can count yourself dead. Believe that you are already dead to the power of sin. Sin has no dominion over you. Your body is not a body of sin.

As you reckon yourself dead to the power of sin, it will cease to have any appeal to you. You will not yield to its temptations. **You are able to prevent sin from reigning in your body.** You do not have to obey its evil desires. Instead you can live as one who has been brought from death to life. **You can offer the parts of your body to God as instruments of righteousness.** You have the ability to do this because you are no longer in bondage to sin.

Say it to yourself and believe it: "I have died to sin. Sin no longer has any hold over me."

> *We were therefore buried with him through baptism into death in order that, just as Christ was raised from the dead through the glory of the Father, we too may live a new life.*
> (Romans 6:4)

Your old life has been put to death with Jesus on the cross. Your water baptism signifies that it was buried with Him. It is so devoid of life that it has been given a funeral service! Whatever belonged to the old life has therefore been buried. Sin, sickness, bondage, failure; all are dead and buried.

Because you were dead and buried with Christ, you have been raised to a glorious new life. This is not an impossibility. He has given you the new life. You are able to live the new life.

Freed From Satan's Power

Satan has no hold over you as he did in your old life. The power with which God raised Jesus from the dead now lives in you!

> *If we have been united with him like this in his death, we will certainly also be united with him in his resurrection.*
> (Romans 6:5)

You were completely identified with Jesus in His whole work of salvation. When He died, you died. When He was buried, your old life was buried. When He was raised, you rose with Him. **It is no longer you who live but Christ who lives in you.** His death is a constant reality in your life. His life is a constant reality in you.

> *Since then, you have been raised with Christ, set your hearts on things above, where Christ is seated at the right hand of God.* (Colossians 3:1)

Jesus has triumphed over all the powers of darkness. He has disarmed them. They are impotent against Him and against you because you live in Him. His victory over demonic forces is your victory. He always, therefore, leads you in His triumphant procession. Always! Because Christ has defeated him, Satan is your defeated enemy. He has no hold or control over your life.

This is not wishful thinking. It is the truth. As you believe it, you will see the evidence.

Immeasurable Power

> *That power is like the working of his mighty strength, which he exerted in Christ when he raised him from the dead and seated him at his right hand in the heavenly realms, far above all rule and authority, power and dominion, and every title that can be given, not only in the present age but also in the one to come.* (Ephesians 1:19-21)

The same power with which Jesus was raised from the dead is at work in you. This is a power so great, nothing can compare with it. It is unlimited, immeasurable. This is the power that has overcome death and all the powers of darkness. This life is at work in you now and every day.

> *And God raised us up with Christ and seated us with him in the heavenly realms in Christ Jesus.* (Ephesians 2:6)

You are already seated in the place of victory. Because you share in the heavenly authority of Jesus you are able to reign in life. You can rule over all of your circumstances, over temptation to sin, over all poverty and need, over sickness and disease, over every evil power through faith in Jesus.

Whatever is under the feet of Jesus is under your feet. You can trample under foot everything that opposes your life in Christ. God sees the end from the beginning. He sees you already living and reigning in Him eternally.

11

Position and Performance

Those who want to live in the faith dimension will learn to live according to their position, rather than their performance.

Failure

You have no doubt noticed that your performance does not always match your position in Christ. Sometimes you sin. You are still prone to failure and many times your thoughts, words and actions are inconsistent with one who lives in Christ.

God does not throw you out of His Kingdom because of this. He is undertaking a programme for your life to transform you from one degree of glory to another. He never starts anything He cannot finish. He has prepared good things for you to walk in as He does this transforming work.

> *May God himself, the God of peace, sanctify you through and through. May your whole spirit, soul and body be kept blameless at the coming of our Lord Jesus Christ. The one who calls you is faithful and he will do it.*
>
> (1 Thessalonians 5:23-24)

Because God is faithful He will ensure that His purpose is brought to fulfilment. **You can afford to have faith in a faithful God.** He does not change His mind. **He will never give up on you.** Even when your performance is less than He desires He still loves you and encourages you.

He is ready to forgive you as soon as you turn to Him in repentance. He knows that you do not demonstrate perfectly a life in Christ, neither is Jesus revealed in every aspect of your life. But the more you put your faith in the revelation of who you are in Christ, the more you can live free from condemnation, fear and failure. You can live as a new creation. You can have confidence to come into God's holy presence with a sincere heart, in full assurance of faith. He is with you always. He will never leave you or forsake you.

All His resources are available to you every moment of the day or night. No matter where you are He is true and His words are for you. You can choose to take hold of Him whenever you desire.

Forgiven and Accepted

God's feelings towards you are of total acceptance, total forgiveness, total approval and perfect love. You do not have to listen to the enemy who falsely accuses you of faults and failings. He wants you to concentrate on them instead of on what Jesus has done for you. Because you do not express the life of Jesus perfectly, he tries to make you feel condemned, to think of yourself as a hopeless failure.

> *Therefore, there is now no condemnation for those who are in Christ Jesus.* (Romans 8:1)

NO CONDEMNATION! NONE WHATSOEVER! NONE!

You do not have to torment yourself with thoughts of your unworthiness before God. **You** now live by the **TRUTH** of **God's Word** and nothing else. **You** do not have to live in defeat and negativity.

> *We are more than conquerors through him who loves us.* (Romans 8:37)

You never have to be defeated by any fear, problem or circumstance. Paul, if anyone, knew what it was to go through enormous trials and difficulties. Yet he could still say at the end of it:

Who shall separate us from the love of Christ? Shall trouble or hardship or persecution or famine or nakedness or danger or sword? ... No, in all these things we are more than conquerors through him who loved us. (Romans 8:35, 37)

Absolutely nothing and no-one can separate you from God's love.

God desires for YOU:

To believe His Word about yourself.
To live a life controlled by His Spirit, resisting sin and walking in righteousness.
To live in His POWER and VICTORY.
To know His Love, Acceptance and Forgiveness.

God wants **you** to look at yourself and at others through His eyes, not your own.

12

Confessing Your Inheritance

When Jesus was teaching the crowds He said:

> *I tell you that men will have to give account on the day of judgement for every careless word they have spoken. For by your words you will be acquitted, and by your words you will be condemned.* (Matthew 12:37)

Each word you speak has significance and importance. Words have the power to place you back under condemnation. With negative words you condemn yourself by your **unbelief**. For instance, if you speak words of failure and defeat about a situation, you cannot at the same time have faith in the power and victory of Christ to change those particular circumstances. If you say: "I fear the worst; it is bound to happen", you do not believe the Scripture which says:

> *In all things God works for the good of those who love him, who have been called according to his purpose.* (Romans 8:28)

Each time you speak negatively of fear and defeat, you are not speaking faith; your words are inconsistent for someone who is in Christ Jesus.

> *Make a tree good and its fruit will be good; or make a tree bad and its fruit will be bad, for a tree is recognised by its fruit.* (Matthew 12:33)

Good fruit comes from a good tree and bad fruit from a bad tree – you cannot have a mixture of the two. See yourself as the tree. God has made **you** good. He has taken hold of **YOUR** life, placed **YOU** in His Son and given **YOU** His Holy Spirit. **You are good in God's eyes.** He has made **YOU** good in order that **YOU** produce **GOOD FRUIT**.

Faith Comes from the Heart

Out of the over-flow of the heart, the mouth speaks.
(Matthew 12:34)

Whatever type of fruit you bear, whether it is good or bad, it originates and stems from the condition of your heart.

The good man brings good things out of the good stored up in him, and the evil man brings evil things out of the evil stored up in him. (Matthew 12:35)

Faith has to begin in your heart and affect your words and actions. You need to have a good heart if you are to produce good fruit; if your heart is full of love, you will speak out words of love. If your heart is full of hope you will speak out words of encouragement.

If your heart is full of faith because you believe what God has done for you, then you will speak the truth about yourself. If you believe and speak it, you can live according to the truth. If you do not speak it, then you will not live it either.

13

Things that Oppose Faith

There are four principal things that undermine the working of faith in your life:

a) Reason

God has given you a mind and intellectual ability. You have the power to reason, but your own thoughts are often contradictory to God's Word. God's thoughts are higher than your thoughts (Isaiah 55:8).

Because reason is a God-given gift, there must be a right way to use it; not to limit faith but to understand what God is saying in His Word and to apply it to our lives so that we make the right decisions with our wills.

You receive revelation from God in your spirit. Your mind then seeks to understand what God has said and applies it.

God's Word will not limit your reason but expand it. You need to have a mind that believes that you can do the same things Jesus did, simply because this is what He says! God can work miracles and healings through you even though that is unreasonable. *God is not opposed to reason; He is simply beyond reason.*

b) Feelings

Your feelings will often contradict what God says in His Word and you will have to choose between what you feel and what God says. When you learn to submit your feelings to the truth, then your feelings will change.

Before you became a Christian you lived by your feelings; that is walking in the flesh, not in the Spirit. You cannot live by faith and live by your feelings which change rapidly. Your faith needs to be constant because it is based in God and His Word.

c) Circumstances

Often your circumstances will seem complex, difficult and at times even impossible. If your faith is in the situation you will disregard the Word of God and His promises which will lead to struggle and failure. As a child of God you must not be ruled by your circumstances. Learn to rule over your circumstances. This involves speaking to mountains and expecting them to be moved.

d) Satan

The devil is your enemy as well as God's enemy. He is opposed to the Word of God and wants to try to undermine your confidence in what God says. He is the Father of lies who kills, steals and destroys. But you have the authority and power in Jesus to withstand him. ***Learn to rebuke and dismiss every thought he sows in your mind which opposes what God says about you and what He is able to do about your circumstances.*** God is truth; Satan is a liar. Who are you going to believe?

The Witness of the Spirit

We have seen that feelings often contradict our faith in God's Word. However, one of the most precious indicators we have of God's will in our lives is often called "the inner witness of the Spirit". Nobody can teach you what this is; you can only learn to distinguish it in your own experience. It is very different from emotional feelings. Usually with the inner witness of the Spirit very little, if any, emotion is involved. You simply know that you know that you know. You would not even be able to say how you know. You just know that God has said something or that He will do some particular thing. There is no need to be anxious or worried. God has everything under His control. He has heard your prayer and has answered you.

14

Victory over the Enemy

When you move in dynamic faith, you are able to exercise authority effectively over Satan and all his powers. You do not allow him to rob you in the way he did before. Jesus describes him as a thief who wants to steal your joy, peace and even undermine your faith by making you feel condemned and out of relationship with the Lord. Learn to resist all his negative and lying accusations. Stand firm against the thoughts he tries to feed into your mind by using the weapons of your warfare which are mighty to the pulling down of strongholds. Take every thought captive to make it obedient to Christ.

> *The weapons we fight with are not the weapons of the world. On the contrary, they have divine power to demolish strongholds. We demolish arguments and every pretension that sets itself up against the knowledge of God, and we take every thought captive to make it obedient to Christ.*
>
> (2 Corinthians 10: 4-5)

You have spiritual authority to pull down the strongholds of wrong thinking in your mind, the attitudes which are inconsistent with the teaching of God's Word, the areas where the enemy still has a foothold in your mind.

You may be aware of some of these strongholds which produce a steady stream of negative, unbelieving or wrong thoughts. It is not enough to parry each wrong thought; you need to come against the stronghold which produces them.

Ask the Holy Spirit to make these clear to you. Then come against them with all your spiritual authority. Having dealt with the negative, fill your mind with the positive truth. God does not want you to have an empty, passive mind, but one that is filled with the positive truth of His Word.

The lies of the enemy are defeated by the truth.

The thief cannot rob you when you stand firm.

Defend yourself against the accusations of the evil one with the shield of faith.

Attack the strongholds of the enemy in your thinking with the spiritual weapons God has given you.

Attack the enemy with the sword of the Spirit which is God's Word.

Stand against his attempts to deceive you by holding fast to God's Word with an honest and good heart.

You have the mind of Christ.

You have authority to overcome the devil;

> *to heal the sick;*
> *to cast out demons;*
> *to set captives free.*

You are able to prevent the enemy from oppressing you by living close to Jesus continually.

15

Jesus' Prayer Promises

Jesus makes a series of astounding promises when He teaches the disciples how to pray:

> *I tell you the truth, anyone who has faith in me will do what I have been doing. He will do even greater things than these, because I am going to the Father.* **And I will do whatever you ask in my name, so that the Son may bring glory to the Father. You may ask me for anything in my name, and I will do it.** (John 14: 12-14)

> **If you remain in me and my words remain in you, ask whatever you wish, and it will be given you.** (John 15:7)

> *You did not choose me, but I chose you and appointed you to go and bear fruit – fruit that will last.* **Then the Father will give you whatever you ask in my name.** (John 15:16)

> **Ask and you will receive, and your joy will be complete.** (John 16:24)

> **I tell you the truth, whatever you bind on earth will be bound in heaven, and whatever you loose on earth will be loosed in heaven.** (Matthew 18:18)

> *I tell you the truth, if you have faith and do not doubt, not only can you do what was done to the fig-tree but also you can say to this mountain, 'Go, throw yourself into the sea' and it will be done.* **If you believe, you will receive whatever you ask for in prayer.** (Matthew 21:21-22)

Notice how often Jesus promises that He will give **whatever** is asked in His name. He does not say it could be yours, or might be yours, but it **shall** be given you! **God always answers prayers of faith.** He is committed to this.

Jesus' idea of faith is very different from that of most Christians. He does not divorce prayer from faith.

> *IF YOU BELIEVE, YOU WILL RECEIVE WHATEVER YOU ASK FOR IN PRAYER.* (Matthew 21:22)

We cannot explain away such a statement. It is emphatic. **Every prayer of faith will be answered by God.**

Using Scripture

It is very important to learn to use the Word of God in your prayers. Jesus said, *"My Words are spirit and life"*. God's Word is truth. It will never fail. God watches over His Word to perform it. If you pray according to the Word of God you are praying according to the will of God.

However, you must be careful not to extract promises from the Bible without taking note of the condition that often goes with the promise. It is no use holding a promise before God if you are not fulfilling the condition He has given.

Faith comes from hearing the Word of God. So your faith will be built up and encouraged as you spend time every day reading and studying the Scriptures and learning to pray over them.

Take a passage of Scripture and make it personal to yourself. Realise that God is speaking directly to you as one of His children. Pray over each phrase, preferably aloud, and ask the Holy Spirit to work that particular truth into your heart and life. You will be amazed that words you have often read will come to life in your spirit in a new way when you learn to pray like this. This is because these words came to you as a personal revelation. The Holy Spirit and the Word are to work together in your life.

16

The Prayer of Faith

Read Mark 11:22-25. Jesus taught His disciples how to pray with faith in these verses.

a) **He tells the disciples to "have faith in God"** – not in their doubts, feelings, reason or problems, but in God. This can be literally translated, *"have the faith of God"*; in other words, the faith that comes from Him.

b) He tells the disciples to **address the problem, speaking to the mountain of need, telling it to be moved**. This is a faith attitude, knowing that you have the authority to address the problem.

c) He points out that when doing this, **the disciple must not doubt in his heart but believe that what he says will happen**. Then it will be done for him. The Christian does not have to move the mountain; only speak to it with faith. Imagine trying to push a mountain into the sea manually with all your might – ridiculous! Speak to it, believing, and **it will be done for you**. Hallelujah!

d) Then you are to ask in prayer, **believing you have already received the answer**. This is the crux of praying with faith. Sometimes you will hear Christians say that they believe that God will answer in the future. That is hope – not faith.

Hope says it **will** happen.

Faith says it **has** happened.

Jesus tells us to believe that we have received the answer to our prayers. Even though there may be nothing to see, you are to believe that you have received your answer.

Now faith is being sure of what we hope for and certain of what we do not see. (Hebrews 11:1)

3) Whenever you pray, it is important to **forgive any who have wronged you**. If you do not forgive others, God will not forgive you and if God does not forgive you then He is unlikely to give to you. He is a God of mercy and has shown His mercy to you in innumerable ways. He therefore expects you to show mercy to others.

When you pray, it is worthwhile pausing to ask yourself what you believe God will do in response to any petitionery prayer. What do you believe will really happen? It is necessary to do this when praying in groups. Everybody may say the "Amen" at the end of a prayer, but how do you know they are agreeing in faith? Sometimes it is good to stop and ask what people believe God will do definitely in response to the prayer. This will show where there is genuine faith and where there is unbelief that needs to be faced.

Again, I tell you that if two of you on earth agree about anything you ask for, it will be done for you by my Father in heaven. (Matthew 18:19)

There is tremendous power in agreeing together, Our heavenly Father will answer when there is true agreement in faith.

17

In the Name of Jesus

What does it mean to pray in the name of Jesus? It is certainly not a question of simply adding His name at the end of a prayer, so that everybody knows it is time to say "Amen"!

> *To pray in the name of Jesus is to pray in the person of Jesus, to pray as He would in your circumstances, with the authority He would exercise.*

You can ask yourself the following questions:

> If Jesus was in my situation what would He pray? – That is what I need to pray.
> What would He believe? – That is what I need to believe.
> How would He address the problem? – That is how I need to address it.

As a believer, the Holy Spirit lives in you to enable you to speak and act in the name of Jesus. Paul says:

> *And whatever you do, whether in word or deed, do it all in the name of the Lord Jesus, giving thanks to God the Father through him.* (Colossians 3:17)

The Will of God

If our prayers are inconsistent with what Jesus would pray, we are not truly praying in His name. Many Christians have been taught to attach the phrase "If it be your will" to the end of their prayers. Nowhere does Jesus teach us to pray in this way. If we pray in His name we will pray according to His will. God's Word reveals what His will is.

The phrase "If it be your will" suggests that you do not know what God's will is; in which case you will be double- minded and cannot expect to receive anything from God. **You can only pray with faith when you know the will of God.** It is important, therefore, to listen to what God is saying in His Word and by His Spirit.

Jesus taught us to pray, *"Your Kingdom come, your will be done on earth as it is in heaven."* Is there sin in heaven? Then God is prepared to forgive those who turn to Him in repentance. Is there sickness in heaven? Of course not. So it is God's purpose to bring healing on earth, that there may be health on earth as in heaven.

In the Garden of Gethsemane Jesus prayed, *"Father, everything is possible for you. Take this cup from me. Yet not what I will, but what you will."* He knew what the will of His Father was, yet in His manhood had to face conflict. He submitted to His Father and went willingly to the cross. When you know the will of God, but are reluctant to accept it, then it is right to surrender by praying, "Not my will but yours be done."

18

Faith Working Through Love

The only thing that counts is faith working through love.
(Galatians 5:6)

Paul makes it clear that if we have faith that is able to move mountains but have not love, we are nothing.

There is no contradiction between a life of faith and a life of love. Just as faith without love is futile in God's sight, so love without faith is similarly empty. **God intends faith to be working through love, and love to be expressed in faith.**

The gift of faith is a gift of the Holy Spirit; the first fruit of the Spirit is love. When you live by faith, walking closely to Jesus, you are living in the One who is love and His love will be increasingly expressed in your life.

Sometimes the life of faith is portrayed as being cold and even heartless. Nothing could be a greater travesty of the truth. We can only please God who is love by a life of faith. So in your life, God wants to bring these two great principles together. **You can walk by faith and live in love.**

God is love. Whatever He does in the lives of His children, He does in love. We have seen that our faith is dependent upon our understanding of who God is. In His love He wants to give to us in every situation. **He wants to care for us, provide for us, protect us, heal us and fill us with Himself.**

Loving Others

Because He is love, He tells us that we too are to love one another with the same love with which He has loved us. At first sight there may seem to be little connection between loving one another and believing God to answer prayer. However, unless we are filled with God's love we will not forgive others when they hurt us and wrong us. Jesus makes it clear that if we do not forgive others God does not forgive us. If we are not forgiven, it does not matter how much we try to believe God, it will seem that He is deaf to our entreaties.

It is also a principle of God's Kingdom that the measure we give is the measure we get back. **If you are not giving to others in love it is difficult to receive.** God's love is expressed in giving and serving. When you pray with faith you know that God wants to answer you; but you also need to be able to receive what He is giving. If you are walking in love then you are an open vessel in which God can easily pour His riches.

In His first epistle, John makes it very clear that your true relationship with God is expressed in your relationship with others, especially with your Christian brethren. Anybody who says that he loves God but does not love his brother is only deceived. He lies and does not know the truth. John further points out that if you do not love the brother you can see, how can you love God who you do not see?

You are called to live in a relationship of love with the Lord and it is within that relationship that He blesses, heals us and answers our prayers. **The evidence of living in relationship with God is not to claim spiritual experiences but to be walking in love for others.** This is not only a question of giving to others, but also of being prepared to receive the love of God through others.

Often God will want to answer your prayers through someone else. He will move in the heart of another believer to give to you, to serve you, to love you, to pray for you. He will use such occasions to speak and minister into your life in the way that is necessary. **But if you are too proud to let any one minister to you, then you could miss the answer to your own prayer!**

To walk in love is therefore to be able to give and to receive in love. How could the Church be the body of love God intends it to be if everybody was giving, but nobody was prepared to receive?

Living in obedience to the Lord gives confidence in prayer. Jesus made it quite clear:

My command is this: love one another.

When you are living in love you know you are obeying the Lord's purpose and can have every confidence that He will express His love to you in giving what you need to receive. If you are walking in mercy and forgiveness towards others, no bitter root will grow up within you to destroy your peace and to block the flow of God's power in your life. Paul tells us:

> *If I have a faith that can move mountains, but have not love, I am nothing.*   (1 Corinthians 13:2)

Faith and Obedience

There is a direct relationship between faith and obedience. When God speaks, He does so as your Lord and is therefore to be obeyed. Faith operates when you do what God tells you to do, even if you feel that you are incapable of doing it. If God has given you a command and you step out in obedience, you will find that He will give you all you need in the situation. He will never ask you to do anything without supplying the resources for you to do it.

Faith is obedience to God's revealed will. It is doing what He says so that His will can be accomplished. One of the most important things for you to do as a Christian is to seek to understand God's will for your life, and His will in your day to day circumstances. You can only fulfil that will by faith.

> *Faith is to be the principle operating in your life so that whatever God says, you will not only hear and agree with Him but will do it!*

19

Faith and Presumption

There is a big difference between these two. The grounds of faith must always be God and what He says in His Word or by His Spirit. People move into presumption when they try to believe God without basing what they believe on what God Himself is saying in that particular situation. **Faith is a response to the initiative of God.**

Presumption takes the initiative away from God so that the believer acts on his own initiative. It is hardly surprising, therefore, that when a Christian moves in presumption he will be disappointed by the results.

The easiest way to describe the difference between faith and presumption is to give you an example. Some years ago I needed a new ministry car, although I did not have the necessary finances to buy one. When I prayed about the matter I knew that God was telling me to go out and order the best car available for the needs of the ministry. This involved getting the biggest station-wagon on the market, as I needed to take a team around with me, together with luggage, books and tapes.

I ordered the car, which would be available six weeks later. After two weeks I was due to go to Australia for a time of ministry and asked the Lord to supply the money before I went so that no debt would be hanging over the ministry while I was away. From an unexpected source the Lord supplied a personal gift that enabled me to pay cash for the car, with an abundance besides. Praise God for His gracious provision! That is an example of faith operating, because I clearly had a word from God telling me to go and order the car.

A young member of my team wanted the Lord to provide a new car for him personally. He thought to himself, "Colin's God is my God. His heavenly Father is my heavenly Father. So if God can supply for Colin, He can supply for me." Unknown to me at the time, he went out and ordered a new car for himself. By the time it was due to be delivered, the necessary money had not been supplied. The young man came to see me in some concern. Lovingly but firmly I pointed out that he had moved in presumption. God had not given him a word, but he had taken the initiative into his own hands.

That is an example of presumption, not faith. When he asked me what he should do, I told him to go to the salesman and be honest. God graciously moved in the man's heart and released him from the contract. He is a God of grace! We all make mistakes; it is important to learn from them!

Disappointments

At times all of us are disappointed by the results of our prayers. As far as we have understood, we have moved in faith, believing we have heard from God and seeking to hold fast to His words of promise. We are perplexed and ask such questions as, "Why didn't God answer me?"

Faith often involves the exercise of authority, speaking to situations as well as to God. Sometimes Christians fail to do this.

At other times they fail to exercise the authority God has given them over the powers of opposition which are seeking to withstand the believer.

Sometimes it becomes apparent later that God's wisdom was greater. There will be many occasions when you will be thankful later that He did not answer your prayer in the way you had thought right at the time. God had some better plan and purpose for you. **Remember that, even when you are disappointed at the results, you are still held in God's perfect love.**

20

Giving and Receiving

Fear is the enemy of faith. Jesus tells us not to be anxious about tomorrow or any of the details of our lives. **We cannot trust Him and remain anxious.** He tells us to seek first the Kingdom of God and His righteousness. Then everything else will be added to us.

God wants you to prosper materially as well as spiritually. There is much controversy as to whether God intends believers to prosper. The Scriptures make it very clear that He does, but not in a worldly, selfish sense. He wants them to prosper, even financially, so that we will have more to give to the work of His Kingdom and to those in need. Those with a poverty mentality have very little to give. If you take your concordance and look up the word 'prosperity' you will be busy for a long time seeing how God intends His people to prosper. Poverty is a curse, not a virtue.

God's generosity to us is a response to our willingness to give first.

> *Give, and it will be given to you. A good measure, pressed down, shaken together and running over, will be poured into your lap. For with the measure you use, it will be measured to you.* (Luke 6:38)

Whatever you give to God, He will give far more back to you. He will not allow you to do anything better than He does! His Kingdom principle is that you give first.

When you were born again, God gave you your rich inheritance in Christ; but you did not receive it until first you had given yourself to Him. You gave your life to Him; He gave His life to you. Not a bad swap!

The Giving Principle

Paul teaches the principle of giving. He says:

> *For you know the grace of our Lord Jesus Christ, that though he was rich, yet for your sakes he became poor, so that you through his poverty might become rich.*
>
> (2 Corinthians 8:9)

Paul makes this statement in the middle of a passage where he is talking about material poverty and prosperity, but it is obviously true of spiritual riches as well. He goes on to teach:

> *Remember this: Whoever sows sparingly will also reap sparingly, and whoever sows generously will also reap generously.* (2 Corinthians 9:6)

This is the same principle Jesus taught: The measure you give is the measure you get back. The more you sow, the more you reap.

What is God's purpose in this?

> *And God is able to make all grace abound to you, so that in all things at all times, having all that you need, you will abound in every good work.* (2 Corinthians 9:8)

God wants all grace to abound to you.
He wants you to have all things at all times.
He wants you to have all that you need.
His reason for all this: so that you will abound in every good work.

Paul explains what this means:

> *You will be made rich in every way so that you can be generous on every occasion.* (2 Corinthians 8:11)

As a believer, He is talking about you. He is not interested in you having material wealth that you can store up for yourself. The resources He makes available to you can be used for the sake of His Kingdom.

There is a cycle that needs to develop in the life of every believer. You give, and God gives more back. You then have more to give and He gives still more back. Then you give still more away and God gives even more than that back to you. And so on. Many, including myself, would testify to the truth of this scriptural principle from personal experience.

Before my wife and I began to operate these principles, we had very little to give away. When we understood that God wanted us to prosper, we could believe Him to give to us more abundantly. As a result we have been able to give immense sums of money away. This is the fruit of seeking first the Kingdom of God. We are concerned to spread the Good News of the Kingdom and to make all our resources of time and money available to God for this purpose.

You can never lose out when you are generous in the way God tells you to be.

Faith Involved in Giving

Often it is an act of faith to give away before seeing the return; but if you are faithful in giving, God will certainly prove faithful in giving back to you. **It is important to sow the seed in fertile soil.** You do not sow seeds in a desert. If you do, the seed will come to nothing. If you give into ministry which God is prospering by the power of His Spirit, that seed will prove abundantly fruitful. The one who gives, as well as the one who receives, will be blessed.

God is a God of grace. He wants to give to His children.

From the fulness of his grace we have all received one blessing after another. (John 1:16)

He gives His everything to those who deserve nothing. You cannot buy His favours. You cannot purchase His blessings.

60

Everything you receive is a work of God's grace. He is teaching you to live by the principles of faith. To give to others continually and faithfully enables you to live in the flow of His giving to you, spiritually and materially. Whenever you receive from Him you are able to give to others; and many thanksgivings ascend to His throne for His glory.

21

The Spirit of Faith

Let There Be Light

The Bible begins with a description of the earth that is impossible for us to imagine.

> *In the beginning God created the heavens and the earth. Now the earth was formless and empty, darkness was over the surface of the deep, and the Spirit of God was hovering over the waters.* (Genesis 1:1-2)

It is impossible for us to imagine the earth being formless and empty. And anyway it was dark; so we would not be able to see what existed. Into this situation God speaks:

> *And God said, "Let there be light," and there was light. God saw that the light was good, and he separated the light from the darkness.* (Genesis 1:3-4)

God simply spoke and immediately light was created. He did not think to Himself: "I wonder what would happen if I spoke to this formless mass. I will try it and see. 'Let there be light.' Oh, that is rather good." No, it was not like that at all. God already conceived in His mind what He would do and simply spoke it into being. When He said that it was good, He was saying that **what had happened was precisely what He had in mind**.

In the first chapter of John's gospel, Jesus is described as the Word of God. Jesus was the Word that went forth from the mouth of God when He created. That Word became a man and lived for a while on the earth.

> *Through him all things were made; without him nothing was*

made that has been made. In him was life, and that life was
the light of man.   (John 1:3-4)

**The same principle operated throughout Jesus' ministry.
He conceived in His mind what was to happen and spoke it
into being.** Often when He healed people it was with a simple
command, *"Be opened"*, *"Your faith has made you well"*, *"Rise
up and walk"*. He also commanded demons to come out of people
with a word. He commanded the wind and the waves and
immediately the storm ceased. He demonstrated His authority and
power through the things He said.

You Can Do Likewise

You have become a Christian because God has spoken over your
life. He has made His light to shine in your heart. Paul says:

> *For God, who said, "Let light shine out of darkness," made
> his light shine in our hearts to give us the light of the
> knowledge of the glory of God in the face of Christ.*
>   (2 Corinthians 4:6)

Once you were in spiritual darkness, but God commanded that
you should not only receive light but that light should shine out of
your darkness. That is His purpose for your life. Jesus said:

> *In the same way, let your light shine before men, that they
> may see your good deeds and praise your Father in heaven.*
>   (Matthew 5:16)

The Lord has given you His Spirit and all the resources of His
Kingdom. Jesus lives in you. Paul says:

> *But we have this treasure in jars of clay to show that this all-
> surpassing power is from God and not from us.*
>   (2 Corinthians 4:7)

The temptation is to concentrate on the jar of clay instead of the treasure within. You will need to remind yourself constantly that **God has put that treasure within you so that you are able to do the same things as Jesus.** Paul continues:

> *It is written: "I believed; therefore I have spoken." With that same spirit of faith, we also believe and therefore speak.*
>
> (2 Corinthians 4:13)

When the Scripture says, *"I believe; therefore I speak"* it refers to God Himself. When He brought creation into being, He believed that what He conceived in His divine mind would come into being as soon as the words left His mouth. When Jesus was ministering to the sick and bound people He believed that He only had to speak the word of command and release and they would be immediately healed and set free.

The amazing thing is that God says to us in His Word that **the same spirit of faith is to operate within you. With that same Spirit of faith you believe and therefore can speak.**

It is important, therefore, to realise that **you are able to speak things into being. You are able to speak healing and release into peoples' lives. You are able to alter the circumstances in your own life by speaking with the Spirit of faith!**

Jesus made it quite clear that He never acted independently from His Father. He tells us, *"Apart from me you can do nothing."* **If we try to speak things into being without first hearing from Him we will be sadly disappointed at the results.** But if we listen to the Holy Spirit's voice speaking to us through scripture and prophetically in prayer, then we are able to speak into being whatever He says He will do. *"With that same spirit of faith, we also believe and therefore speak."*

The life of faith is not only expressed in prayer to God, but in our willingness to exercise the authority given us by speaking into situations in His name.

22

The Gift of Faith

Not every born again Spirit-filled Christian lives by faith, although this is what God intends. Not all exercise the spirit of faith by believing and speaking things into being. Jesus says that from the overflow of the heart the mouth speaks. One with a spirit of faith will speak words of faith. He is able to do this because he has received revelation of the truth of God's Word which enables him to live in utter dependence on what God says.

It could be said that the one who lives in dynamic faith has received the gift of faith.

We need to obey the command in Scripture to earnestly desire the spiritual gifts. One of these is the gift of faith (1 Corinthians 12:9). Some people interpret this as a momentary gift that God gives in a particularly difficult situation, inspiring the Christian to believe what he would normally find impossible to believe.

None of the other gifts are withdrawn when they are not in use. The one who prophesies does not prophesy continually, but he can exercise this gift at any time. The same is true of those God uses to heal, speak in tongues, and so on. The gift is there to be used whenever the need arises.

It is the same with the gift of faith. Just as God wants you to use the gift of tongues daily so that the Spirit of God can pray in you and through you and for you, so He also wants you to operate in faith and put it into operation daily.

Those who use this gift of faith trust God on a totally different level. This does not necessarily mean that everything is going to be easy. Such faith is exercised in the middle of opposition, worldly unbelief and immense problems. **You learn to develop your use of the gift by trusting God despite the circumstances. You have a faith which enables you to overcome and see situations transformed.**

Living a life like this is much more than saying, "I believe in

Jesus" or "I believe in God's love". It is learning to trust Jesus in every situation, to trust in the Father's love continually. This is the dimension of faith in which God wants you to live. It is intensely practical.

Whether it is described as having a gift of faith or a spirit of faith, there is no doubt that it is possible for a person to experience a definite event which produces a number of dynamic results in his life. It is a work of God's grace in the heart and life of the believer.

Earnestly Desire the Gift

How and when can such an event take place?

First, the believer must want this. There needs to be a cry from his heart which expresses the desire to walk more closely with Jesus and to live in the dimension of faith which will be truly pleasing to Him. Only then can the words of Jesus be fulfilled in his life:

> *I tell you the truth, anyone who has faith in me will do what I have been doing.* *He will do even greater things than these, because I am going to the Father. And I will do whatever you ask in my name, so that the Son may bring glory to the Father. **You may ask me for anything in my name, and I will do it.*** (John 14:12-14)

As soon as there is this genuine desire, God will answer the cry of the heart. Of course, the believer will experience testing because only in this way will he learn how to persevere and to hold fast to the Word of God with an honest and good heart.

The Benefits

We can list some of the benefits of this event as follows:

A fresh revelation of God's Word, inspiring faith.

Greater submission to the authority of God's Word.
Determination to stand on God's Word despite difficulties.
A closer walk with the Lord.
A more victorious life.
Personal revelation of his position in Christ.
Freedom from condemnation.
Dependence on God's grace.
A consciousness of God's holiness, reflected in his life-style.
Access into the Holy of Holies with "a sincere heart, in full assurance of faith".
A more vital prayer life.
More answers to prayer.
Effective exercise of authority over the powers of darkness.
Victory over Satan and all his works.
Faith for healing.
Miracles.

You need the spirit of faith.

You need the gift of faith to be operating in your life every day.

And this is what God wants for you.

Make the decision to live in the faith dimension.

Reach out to God for the gift of faith.

You will see many answers to prayer.

You will begin to rule over the adverse circumstances in your life.

You will reign in life as a child of His Kingdom.

23

The Five-fold Confession of Faith

1. – Learn to speak the Word to yourself.
2. – Learn to speak the Word to God.
3. – Learn to speak the Word to Satan.
4. – Learn to speak the Word to other believers.
5. – Learn to speak the Word to the world.

1. Speak the Word to Yourself

A practical exercise
It is good to learn to speak the Word of God out aloud to yourself.
If you can't do this, you are not going to find it easy to speak it
out to others! Psalm 103 begins:

> *Praise the Lord, O my soul; all my inmost being, praise his
> holy name!*

David is speaking faith to himself. He is saying: "Come on
David, get your eyes off yourself and your problems and start
looking to God, praising Him for all He has done for you." He
then voices five good reasons for praising the Lord:

> – *He forgives all my sins;*
> – *He heals all my diseases;*
> – *He redeems my life from the pit;*
> – *He crowns me with love and compassion;*
> – *He satisfies my desires with good things.*

David's praise increases as he recounts the Lord's goodness to
him. By the end of the psalm, his praise is no longer an act of the
will; it is rising spontaneously and eagerly from deep within his

soul. He even cries out to the heavenly host to join his proclamation of praise. This psalm is a perfect illustration of how praise can transform us from being self-absorbed and inward-looking, into people of worship, filled with the wonder and awe of God's love for us.

Applying the Word Personally

You can only declare God's Word if you know His Word! A person can read Scripture without appreciating that these words contain life and Spirit; they are a source of healing to his whole being. When you come across any phrase which speaks of being "in Christ", write it down in a personal form. Know that God is speaking about you because He has placed you "in Christ". For instance,

> *"There is now no condemnation for those who are in Christ Jesus"*,

now becomes,

> *"There is now no condemnation for me because I am in Christ Jesus"*.
> (Romans 8:1)

I am not encouraging you to change to meaning of Scripture, but apply it to yourself in the first person singular. This will help you to realise more readily that God is speaking to you in a direct, personal way – about your new life in Him! The Holy Spirit will recall these familiar Scriptures in your hour of need, the right word for the right occasion.

I used to be a very fearful person. Sometimes fear would grip me to such an extent I was unable to act upon what God was telling me. I soon learned to quote aloud to myself: "Colin, *God has not given you a spirit of fear, but of power, love and self control*" (2 Timothy 1:7). As I listened to the truth of these words I went forward confident in God, rather than paralysed by my fears.

There are always several verses of Scripture relevant to your particular need at any given moment. I did not wait until my fear went before I moved confidently in God; I learned to act on God's Word because I knew His truth is greater than my fear. God always, but always, honours His Word. Jesus is the Living Word of God.

– So then, confess the Word to Yourself.

2. Speak the Word to God

Pray according to the Word of God. God always honours His Word; He cannot break it. The whole universe would collapse if God went back on his Word; for He not only created by speaking His Word, He sustains His creation by His Word. When you pray according to God's Word, you can be sure you are praying according to His will and purpose.

> *My God will meet all your needs according to his glorious riches in Christ Jesus.* (Philippians 4:19)

These glorious riches are your inheritance because you are a co-heir with Christ. It is God's will to supply your every need out of His glorious riches in Christ. When a need arises in your life, whether it is spiritual, physical or material, you can pray to your Father, **knowing it is His will** to supply all your needs.

There are many promises in Scripture; each one of them is for YOU now you are in Christ. Do not reason **how** God will answer; simply receive the word by faith and believe Him to fulfil what He has promised.

God has declared many promises to you through His Word. You can pray, fully expecting these promises to be fulfilled. He will not fail to honour His Word to you; even though sometimes you will have to persist and persevere in faith until you see the answer. He cannot fail to honour His Word to you!

If you have children who do not know the Lord, pray according to the promises He gives you in the Word about your children. If you need healing, pray according to His promises of healing. As you pray, always listen to what God is revealing to you by His Spirit. He will speak words of faith to your heart.

It is not a question of having faith in the promises, but of having faith in the One who gives you the promises. Once you know God to be utterly faithful, you will also come to see that His Word must also be totally reliable. God is at one with His Word. As you get to know God, these promises will become more than words on a page, they will become part of your very being, the treasure stored up within you.

– So then, confess the Word to God in prayer.

3. Speak the Word of God to Satan

This does not mean you have a conversation with the enemy. He is the father of lies and is only out to deceive you. His greatest desire is to destroy your faith in God and His Word. So when you confess the Word of God to Satan, you are **dismissing** him, not having a conversation with him.

Jesus did the same thing: When He was tempted in the wilderness, He counter-acted Satan's temptations with words of Scripture. When Satan tries to tempt you, destroy your peace, accuse you or fill you with doubt, answer him as Jesus did: *"Away from me Satan, for it is written…"*

You cannot do this unless you know the Word of God for yourself. There is no excuse for believers to live in ignorance of the Scriptures. Read your Bible and mark the verses which encourage you and build up your faith. The Book of Hebrews talks of the Word of God as being *"sharper than any two-edged sword"*. A sword is a weapon of attack as well as of defence. Quote aloud God's Word in the face of the enemy and he has no choice but to flee from you (James 4:7).

– So then, confess the Word to the enemy.

4. Speak the Word of God to Other Believers

God wants you to be an encourager. He has not called you to live in isolation; you are a member of His Body, His Chosen People. You are to love others, to care for them, forgiving when necessary, and to pray with them.

> *For anyone who does not love his brother, whom he has seen, cannot love God, whom he has not seen.* (1 John 4:20)

These words are clear and hard-hitting. It is easy to look at your brother and see his faults, yet God's command to you is uncompromising: **Whoever loves God must also love his brother.** God wants you to look at your brothers and sisters with His love; to see that you cannot judge them because Christ died for them as well as for you.

> *If you have any encouragement from being united with Christ, if any comfort from his love, if any fellowship with the Spirit, if any tenderness and compassion, then make my joy complete by being like-minded, having the same love, being one in spirit and purpose. Do nothing out of selfish ambition or vain conceit, but in humility consider others better than yourselves.* (Philippians 2:1-3)

Nothing could be more practical. In the interest of your brother build him up in his faith. Do not destroy him with words of criticism and judgement. When a brother is in need, you can encourage him through directing him to the truth.

Again, this is not the mechanical act of quoting an applicable Scripture at him. You are to be sensitive to his need; Scripture tells us to rejoice with those who rejoice, and mourn with those who mourn. This does not mean you wallow in their problems, but that you minister gently and speak the truth to them.

Fellowships and churches would be transformed if Christians sought to build one another up in the Word instead of destroying each other by judgement and criticism. God does not want His Church, His own Body here on earth, divided with jealousy, anger, bitterness, criticism and quarrelling. He wants His Church to have the unity of His Spirit, peace with God, and peace with one another.

As I have loved you, so you must love one another. All men will know that you are my disciples if you love one another.

(John 13:34-35)

Paul instructs us to:

Let the word of Christ dwell in you richly as you teach and admonish one another with all wisdom, and as you sing psalms, hymns and spiritual songs with gratitude in your hearts to God.

(Colossians 3:16)

– So then, encourage one another through the Word of God.

5. Speak the Word of God to the World

You are surrounded by people who do not know the Lord! What they need is not your opinions or philosophies, but the Word of God. Again, this is not a question of quoting repentance Scriptures at them!

Speaking the Word of God to them means that you first ask God to give you the right word for the situation. It may be a word of Scripture, or a prophetic word. It may even be a question that God leads you to ask, which opens up a fruitful conversation. Whatever it is, you are sharing the truth of God with them and the Word will be very much a part of it.

The promises of Scripture are not for unbelievers and you may have to point this out to them. You can show them how they can come into a relationship with Christ; these promises then become their inheritance also. Allow Him to lead you, to guide you and to put into your mouth the right words to speak. If you are open to the leading of the Holy Spirit, He will do that!

...Do not worry about what to say or how to say it. At that time you will be given what to say, for it will not be you speaking, but the Spirit of your Father speaking through you.

(Matthew 10:19-20)

– So then, confess the Word of God to the world.

73

All Five at Once

I haven't listed the Five-fold Confession of Faith in any order of priority; each one needs to be applied to your life in equal measure, at the same time. You will find that as you confess the truth in this way, His Words will become more firmly rooted and established in your own heart and mind. You will then speak with greater clarity and confidence.

As God's child, you are rich beyond measure. The inheritance God has given you cannot be earned; it can only be received through faith with thanksgiving. **God has not withheld any good thing from you; this wonderful inheritance is for YOU to ENJOY NOW!** Remember:

"I Can't" is unbelief;
"I Won't" is disobedience;
"I Can" is faith;
"I Will" is obedience.

God is calling you to live a life of faith and obedience; if you answer the calling, you will experience life in all its fulness.

24

Helping the Weak

The commands of Scripture are clear. We are to:

Accept him whose faith is weak, without passing judgement...   (Romans 14:1)

We who are strong ought to bear with the failings of the weak and not to please ourselves. Each of us should please his neighbour, to build him up.   (Romans 15:1)

Never accuse someone of not having received an answer to prayer or a healing they need because they don't have enough faith. That may well be true, but it is your responsibility to build them up in faith and encourage them. "You don't have enough faith" is a swift demolition job which confirms a person in their defeat.

Jesus told the disciples their failure to heal was the result of **their** unbelief, not the unbelief of the boy's father!

If you have faith that you see is lacking in another, seek to help them, not demolish them! Sensitively encourage the person to be open with God about their fear, their doubts, their sense of failure and inadequacy. Encourage them by reminding them that the Lord will forgive all of this as they lay it before Him.

Show them that they need to receive a word of faith from God. Ask the Holy Spirit to speak such a word to their heart knowing that faith comes from hearing God's word. Be prepared to be His instrument in speaking such a word to them by listening yourself to what He is saying.

Avoid taking out your own frustration on others. Remember it is easy for you as a by-stander to know what is right. But you are not in their position. Everything may seem to be very dark if the one you are seeking to help is faced by a grave situation. They may feel they are in a dark tunnel. You can point them to the light at the end of the tunnel and sensitively lead them out into that light. But don't try to rush them faster than they are able to go. Keep encouraging them, even when they become despondent.

And remember, you respond particularly to encouragement; but you hate being judged or criticised. Well, do to others as you would have them do to you.

Weakness

Some think that it is wrong for a person seeking to live by faith to admit any personal weakness. Clearly such an attitude is not in line with Scripture. Paul says:

> *I will not boast about myself, except about my weaknesses.*
> (2 Corinthians 12:5)

He had good reason for saying this. The Lord had told him personally:

> *My grace is sufficient for you, for my power is made perfect in weakness.*   (2 Corinthians 12:9)

And so he concludes:

> *Therefore I will boast all the more gladly about my weaknesses, so that Christ's power can rest upon me.*
> (2 Corinthians 12:9)

Jesus hated hypocrisy but loved honesty. There is no point in being anything other than honest with the Lord. He is the Author and Perfecter of our faith. So if we are lacking in faith ourselves, there is no point in trying to disguise this with acts of bravado or the endless repetition of faith formulae. Be honest with God, seek His forgiveness for your unbelief and ask Him for the word of faith you need.

Recognising your own weakness encourages you to depend all the more on Him. In that way His power is made perfect in your weakness.

And help others to see that they do not need to fear being honest with God about what He knows anyway. He alone can forgive unbelief and inspire faith.

At no time does He condemn the one who lives in Him. So be sure you do not heap condemnation onto others. See yourself as one who has the responsibility to build and encourage faith.

On occasions you will have to be exceedingly patient with others while this process is taking place, just as God has often had to be patient with you! That patience is a fruit of the Holy Spirit. Frustration, condemnation and judgement certainly are not.

Let all your words and actions be an expression of love towards the one you wish to help. Look at that person in their dilemma with the compassion of Jesus, with His longing to help, not in judgement.

25

Living in God's Power

God's Kingdom is ordered by divine principles. It is a Kingdom of order, whereas Satan's dominion is full of chaos and disorder.

If we want to receive God's best we need to understand these principles. **We cannot expect God to work in our lives in any other way than that which He promises in His Word.**

We all want God's power in our lives. Jesus promises, *"You will receive power when the Holy Spirit comes upon you."* Paul also says that the Kingdom of God is not a matter of talk but of power. The Greek word used for power in both these Scriptures is *dunamis* which means mighty power. Our English word dynamite comes from this Greek word and gives us some indication of the explosive effect a release of God's power has in the circumstances of our lives.

> *This is the power God released when He spoke creation into being.*
> *This is the power we see operating in the ministry of Jesus.*
> *This is the power God used to raise Jesus from the dead.*
> *This is the power God has placed in your life by the Holy Spirit.*

·You have the same power in you as Jesus had in Him in the days of His humanity. It is for this reason that Jesus said to the disciples, *"You will do the same things I have done when the Spirit comes on you."*

We may have the same power but why do we not always get the same results as Jesus did?

Authority

There is another word, *exousia*, which is sometimes translated power but really means authority. Jesus had authority. This was recognised even by his opponents. Never had they seen anyone preach or act with such authority. They wanted to know where He got such authority from.

Jesus was able to release the power of God into situations in the way He did because He exercised the authority His Father had given Him. The exercise of that authority depended on His submission to God.

Submission

Jesus made it clear:

> *I have not come to do my own will but the will of Him who sent me. I speak no words of my own but only the words He gives me to speak. But he who sent me is reliable, and what I have heard from him I tell the world.* (John 6:38, 8:28)

> *I can do nothing of myself but I do only the things I see my Father doing. I judge only as I hear, and my judgement is just, for I seek not to please myself but him who sent me.* (John 5:30)

> *My decisions are right, because I am not alone. I stand with the Father who sent me.* (John 8:16)

In other words the exercise of authority in Jesus' ministry came as a result of His submission to His Father's authority. He was always obedient and submissive, never taking matters into His own hands, but sensitive to what His Father was saying.

When such submission is expressed in our lives we are acting in obedience. That gives us confidence to exercise the authority God has given us as believers and therefore to see the power of God at work in our circumstances.

Submission to the authority of God enables us to act in faith.

Righteousness

However, there are things that try to undermine our faith. We lose our confidence before God if we are walking in sin instead of righteousness. Jesus demonstrated a perfect faith, which is why He is the Author and Perfecter of our faith. He could express perfect faith because He always walked in righteousness. He always obeyed His Father. He always did the will of God.

So we see in Jesus that there is a progression. He walked in righteousness which enabled Him to live by faith, which enabled Him to exercise authority, which released the power of God into situations.

God intends that same progression to work in your life. **Walk in right relationship with Jesus, obedient to His Word. This will give you confidence to expect Him to answer your prayers and enable you to live and pray with faith. That faith will be expressed in the use of the authority God has given you; and when you move in God's authority power is released into your circumstances.**

Righteousness – Faith – Authority – Power!

That is God's order.

It is not a question only of receiving power from God but of seeing this order operating in our lives to ensure that His power is used effectively.